KEEPSAKE CRAFTS

RIBBONS
& BOWS

KEEPSAKE CRAFTS

RIBBONS & BOWS

HILARY MORE

B.T. Batsford Ltd • London

First published in Great Britain by
B.T. Batsford Ltd.
4 Fitzhardinge Street
London W1H OAH

Copyright © 1994 Quarto Publishing plc

A QUARTO BOOK

ISBN 0-7134-7612-5

A catalogue record for this book is available
from the British Library.

This book was designed and produced by
Quarto Publishing plc
The Old Brewery
6 Blundell Street
London N7 9BH

Senior editor Sally MacEachern
Editor Jane Royston
Senior art editor Amanda Bakhtiar
Designer Alyson Kyles
Photographers Chas Wilder, Paul Forrester
Illustrator Elsa Godfrey
Art director Moira Clinch
Editorial director Sophie Collins

Typeset by Poole Typesetting, Bournemouth
Manufactured in Hong Kong by Regent
Publishing Services Ltd
Printed in China by
Leefung-Asco Printers Ltd

CONTENTS

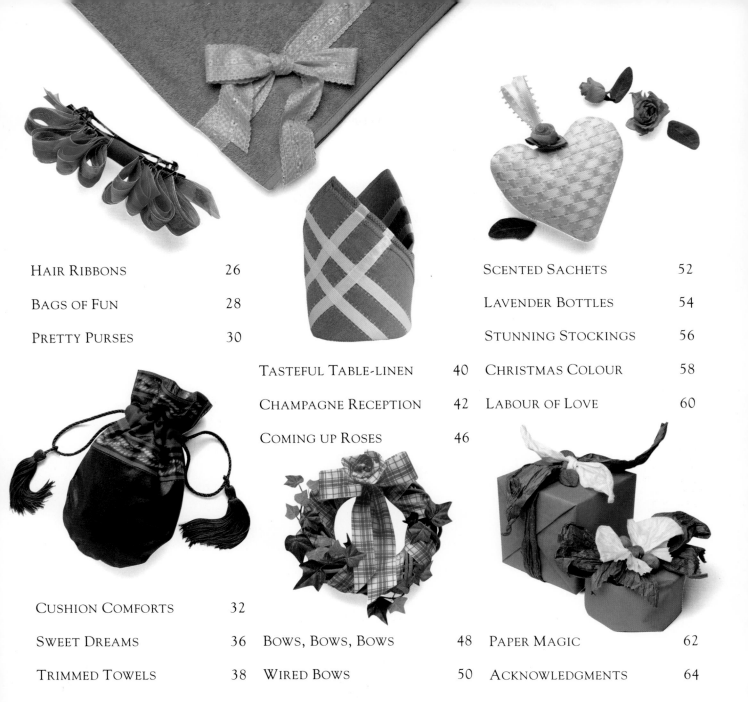

INTRODUCTION

Ribbons have been used through the ages to decorate clothes and furnishings. They are one of the quickest ways of enlivening a garment or household item and, nowadays, with the huge range of ribbons available, it has become even easier to pick just the right ones for your needs.

With the advent of sophisticated machines and computers, ribbon making and printing has been turned into a fine art and ribbons come in an impressive range of widths, materials and designs. Before you begin, have a good look at all the different types of ribbons on the market, pick those most suited to your project and then decide on the pattern and design.

Ribbons can be sewn or glued in position, woven to make a fabric, used as an embroidery thread or simply as a substitute for string. It is important to match your method of attaching the ribbon to the item that you are decorating. Fabric

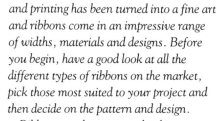

ribbons can be hand or machine-sewn in place, with their ends snipped diagonally or into inverted "V" shapes to prevent fraying. Craft or paper ribbon, on the other hand, will not fray, and can be cut, stuck and curled into shape.

As you will see from the ribbon samples shown here, the wonderful array of colours and designs means that it is never hard to find a ribbon that matches your project perfectly.

SINGLE-FACE SATIN RIBBONS

Single-face satin ribbons come in a good range of widths. They have one shiny and one dull side, and come in a wide range of plain colours and printed patterns. Single-face ribbons also sometimes have picot or metallic edges.

DOUBLE-FACE SATIN RIBBONS

Double-face satin ribbons are shiny on both sides, and are slightly thicker than the single-face variety. They are available in a good selection of plain colours, sometimes with picot or decorative edges.

POLYESTER RIBBONS

Polyester ribbons are found in an impressive range of plain colours, printed patterns and finishes, (such as crêpe), and can be combined with metallic strips or woven as tartans.

GROSGRAIN RIBBONS

Grosgrain ribbons are strong and firm with a distinctive cross-wise rib. They come in a variety of plain colours, as well as some printed or embroidered stripes and patterns. They can also have satin stripes.

TAFFETA RIBBONS

Flat and matt with a woven design, taffeta ribbons are available in many colours. They may also have a water-marked finish such as moiré, or a picot or metallic edge. Nylon taffeta is available in some wonderful gingham checks.

VELVET RIBBONS

Velvet ribbons have a raised pile and can be made in nylon or cotton. They are available as single- or double-face ribbons.

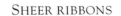

JACQUARD RIBBONS

Jacquard ribbons, woven in a similar style to the fabric of the same name, have a slightly raised design. This is often floral, but can also be geometric or metallic. Jacquard ribbons also sometimes have a picot edge.

METALLIC RIBBONS

Metallic ribbons are woven from lurex and similar metallic fibres, and come in a variety of finishes from sheer to grosgrain.

SHEER RIBBONS

Perfect for making ribbon roses, sheer, light, organdie ribbons can be printed or left plain. Some sheer ribbons have decorative or satin edges, or satin stripes running down the centre.

CRAFT RIBBONS

Also known as florists' ribbons, craft ribbons are really strips of fabric, which have been given a finish to prevent the edges from fraying when cut. This finish makes them unwashable, and therefore unsuitable for some purposes. Craft ribbons come in many plain colours and a huge range of patterns.

EMBELLISHED RIBBONS

Embellished ribbons have a plain surface which is decorated with beads and sequins, making the ribbons perfect for use on party or bridal wear.

PAPER RIBBONS

Paper ribbons are tightly twisted along their length, and can be unwound totally or just in certain sections to arrange into different effects. Fine paper ribbons wound on to spools are also available.

WIRE-EDGED RIBBONS

Wire-edged ribbons have a fine, flexible wire woven along both edges. Once arranged into bows or shapes, the ribbons will retain their position indefinitely. One or both of the wires can be removed to create softer effects.

MATERIALS

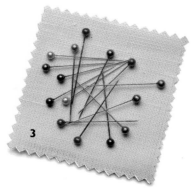

Most of the projects in this book require very little in the way of specialist materials, but there are a few basic items that you will need. If you do not already have these at home, you will be able to buy them from local shopping centres or specialist craft suppliers. For most of the projects, the important point is to choose the materials to match the ribbons you are using. Bear in mind, too, the use that the finished item will undergo when using adhesives and interfacing, for example, as you may need to use a stronger glue or a heavier-weight interfacing if the item will receive a reasonable amount of wear and tear.

PINS AND NEEDLES
You will need a good selection of pins and needles.

1 Fine quilting needles are extremely useful. **2** Curved needles are ideal for stitching ribbons to awkward shapes. **3** Pins with coloured heads are easy to see.

THREADS
Your choice of thread will depend on the type and colour of ribbon you are using.

1 Metallic and iridescent threads add texture and interest. **2** Cotton threads can be chosen to match a colour scheme.

FUSIBLE INTERFACING
Fusible interfacing is used as a base for ribbon weaving - ribbons can be fused to one side of the interfacing and held in position to form a "fabric". Interfacing is available in light, medium and heavy weights.

SCISSORS
You will need several types of scissors for working with ribbons.
1 Choose a large, sharp pair of scissors for general cutting purposes, such as cutting out paper ribbon, patterns and fine wires when making ribbon roses (see page 10).
2 A small pair of scissors with sharp points is vital for cutting out small pieces and intricate corners.

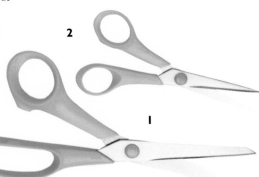

ROSES & ROSETTES

Ribbon roses look marvellous, whether grouped together in a vase or used to augment table decorations and presents - the possibilities are endless. The finished result will depend to a great extent on the type of ribbon that you use. Try sheer ribbon for tight, well-formed roseheads, or double-face satin ribbon for a looser interpretation. Roses can also be created from wire-edged ribbon.

Ribbon rosettes can be made from almost any type of ribbon, as they are simply gathered along one ribbon edge and pulled up into shape. To create a pompon, stick two rosettes back to back around a length of ribbon.

RIBBON ROSE ON A STEM

For each rose you will need 75 cm (30 in) of 40 mm (1½ in) wide sheer ribbon, 50 cm (20 in) of craft wire and one stem wire with green tape to cover the stem.

1 Bend over the top of the stem wire to form a loop, and hold the craft wire at the base of the loop. Lay the end of the ribbon over the loop and wrap round with craft wire to secure it.

2 Bring the ribbon up and wrap it around the stem two or three times to create the centre of the rose.

3 Begin folding the ribbon away from the centre and diagonally forward, catching it at the base each time with the craft wire. At first, fold the ribbon only slightly and wrap tightly, but then, as you work, fold more deeply and ease in more ribbon with each fold to open out the flower.

4 When the rose is the required size, bring the end of the ribbon down to the base of the flower, and bind round this to secure. Position the end of the stem binding tape directly under the rosehead. Bind the stem, attaching the tape at the base.

WIRE-EDGED RIBBON ROSE

For a large rose, cut a 100 cm (40 in) length of wired ribbon.

I Fold the cut edge of the ribbon away from you at an angle of 45°. Now fold the ribbon horizontally towards you, keeping the edges even.

2 Continue to fold, making sure that you always fold away from you at a 45° angle

and that when you fold towards you, you pull the front flap forwards to make a square as shown above.

3 As you fold, try to pull the outside edge of the ribbon slightly tighter than the inner edge.

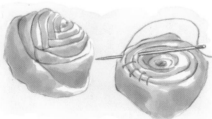

4 When you reach the end of your ribbon, use your fingers to open out the centre of the rose into a rounded flower. Hand sew the ribbon end at the base, and continue stitching as necessary to hold the rose shape.

In order to fill out the gap left underneath, push a small piece of cotton wool up into the back of the rose to hold the shape. Oversew the edges to keep the cotton wool in place.

RIBBON ROSETTE

Take a piece of ribbon approximately 50 cm (20 in) in length. Beginning with a knot, run a line of gathering stitches along one straight edge of the ribbon. Pull up the thread to form the rosette, and fasten it off securely.

POMPONS

To make a pompon, gather up two rosettes and glue them together, back to back (see page 46).

RIBBON WEAVING

Ribbon weaving is similar to traditional weaving, but uses ribbon lengths instead of yarn. It provides a firm, beautifully textured fabric from which all sorts of different items can be cut and stitched. The easiest way to weave ribbons is over a background of fusible interfacing. Once the ribbons are all in place, simply fuse them to the interfacing with a warm iron.

When weaving with ribbons, the vertical ribbons are the warp threads, while the weft refers to the ribbons that are woven from side to side across the vertical ribbons. The finished pattern can be made simple or complex by using different weaving sequences; and also by mixing and matching different ribbon styles and widths in the same piece of work.

Ribbon weaving is simple to learn. You don't need any complicated equipment, and the finished "fabric" can be used to make cushion covers, bags, cloths and many other items.

PLAIN WEAVE

Work with satin-edged 22 mm (⅞ in) wide grosgrain ribbon in two colours.

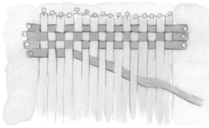

Lay the vertical ribbons out flat, side by side, alternating the colours. Working with the same ribbons horizontally, weave the first row under one, over one, under one, over one, and so on, to the end of the row. In the second row, weave the ribbon over one, under one, over one, under one, and so on, to the end of the row. The result will be smooth, plain-woven ribbon fabric.

PLAIN WEAVE USING THREE COLOURS

By mixing together two different ribbon widths – 16 mm (⅝ in) and 6 mm (¼ in) – and three different colours, you will achieve a totally different effect.

Use the same plain-weave method described left, weaving the horizontal ribbons alternately over and under the vertically placed ribbons.

TUMBLING-BLOCKS WEAVE

Team up two different pinks, both 20 mm (¾ in) wide, with a 16 mm (⅝ in) wide cream ribbon to re-create this typical patchwork design.

1 Lay out the vertical ribbons, and weave the horizontal ribbons through them. In the first row, work over one, under one, over two, under one, over two, and so on, to the end of the row. In the second row, work under one, over two, under one, over two, and so on, to the end, and in the third row work over two, under one, over two, under one and so on.

DIAGONAL WEAVE

Use a mix of three different-coloured ribbons for this diagonal weave – combine a plain 22 mm (⅞ in) wide satin ribbon with two 22 mm (⅞ in) wide satin-edged grosgrain ribbons.

Lay out the vertical ribbons as before. Weave the first horizontal ribbon under two, over two, under two, over two, and so on, to the end of the row. In the second row, work under one, over two, under two, over two, and so on, to the end of the row. Weave the third row over two, under two, over two, and so on, to the end. In the fourth row, work over one, under two, and so on, to the end of the row. Repeat these rows for the whole area to form the diagonal effect.

2 Finally, thread the 16 mm (⅝ in) cream ribbon diagonally to create the pattern.

CLASSIC CARDIGAN

Extra-wide patterned ribbon is ideal for enlivening plain knitted fabric to give it a new lease of life and a totally different look.

Transform a plain, long-line cardigan with ribbon to make a stylish addition to your wardrobe. You could either update a knit that you discarded long ago as boring and old-fashioned, or begin with a new one. Adding ribbon is the ideal way to smarten up a cheap, shop-bought jersey to make you really stand out in a crowd.

The look that you create will depend on your choice of ribbon. Use a wide ribbon with a distinctive *haute-couture* pattern such as the one shown here, and add it to the front and pockets of the cardigan. Begin by laying two strips centrally down both fronts, from the shoulder seams (allowing a little extra ribbon at the top for turning under later), and tuck the bottom ends neatly inside each front pocket.

To hold the ribbon ready for stitching, cut a piece of fusible interfacing to the same length and just under the width of the ribbon. Place the interfacing centrally under each strip and fuse it in place using an iron on a medium setting. Turn under the ribbon ends in

Strips of ribbon from shoulder to pocket, with ribbon on the pocket tops, completely transforms this basic cardigan.

line with the shoulder seams to neaten the top edges, and then hand sew down each side of the ribbon to secure it. Alternatively, work a loose zigzag stitch on a sewing machine. Take care when doing this, as knitting is such a flexible fabric that, if the stitches are too tight, they will snap or may pull the cardigan. Complete the decoration with a band of ribbon applique across the fronts of the pockets.

You could also add ribbon cuffs to your cardigan, or a simple band or bands of ribbon around each sleeve. To make a finishing touch, why not change the buttons too? As this type of ribbon is extra-wide, you can use it to make a set of matching covered buttons – follow the manufacturer's instructions for these, and then stitch them down the front of your cardigan in the usual way.

Make neat folds where the garment line changes direction, and turn under the raw ends of the ribbon at the top in line with the shoulder seams, and at the bottom to align with the hem edges.

You can give extra definition to the waistcoat with three pairs of diagonally folded loops of ribbon, evenly spaced on

UP FRONT

Use ribbon in a pretty floral design, with co-ordinating buttons, to decorate an uninteresting waistcoat. You could choose stronger ribbon colours for an even more striking effect.

A simply styled waistcoat never goes out of fashion, and makes an indispensable addition to any wardrobe. A waistcoat is neat enough just to wear over a shirt, perhaps in combination with a smart tailored skirt or a pair of trousers, or can be slipped under a jacket or a heavy, blanket-type swirling cape for a "layered" fashion look that is also very warm!

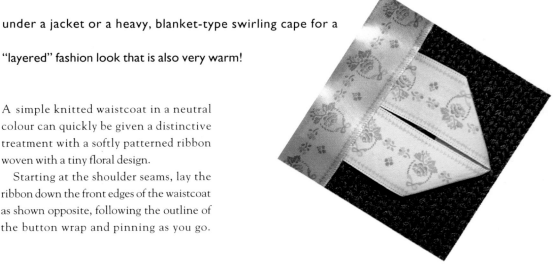

A simple knitted waistcoat in a neutral colour can quickly be given a distinctive treatment with a softly patterned ribbon woven with a tiny floral design.

Starting at the shoulder seams, lay the ribbon down the front edges of the waistcoat as shown opposite, following the outline of the button wrap and pinning as you go.

either side of the button wrap. Fold and press each piece of ribbon to provide a pointed edge, and tuck the opposite ends under the vertical ribbons.

Hand sew all the ribbons in place with invisible stitches around the edges, being careful to let the knitted fabric move under the appliqué. The buttons on the waistcoat may now look out of place against the new arrangement, so swap them for pretty buttons which echo the floral feel of the ribbon, and you will be ready to go!

This type of ribbon decoration need not be restricted simply to waistcoats. A collarless jacket would also lend itself beautifully to this treatment, and you could even add a band of the same ribbon to a hat, and ribbon to shoes, to create a really spectacular "special-occasion" outfit.

Even when the waistcoat is worn under a jacket or coat, the ribbon will highlight its outline and provide a splash of colour.

SNAPPY DRESSER

What could be more appealing than this bright tartan waistcoat? It would give any plain outfit a lift, and

could be worn through the day as a casual accessory, or over a simple black dress during the evening to

provide a dramatic splash of colour. Add a matching bow tie to complete the look.

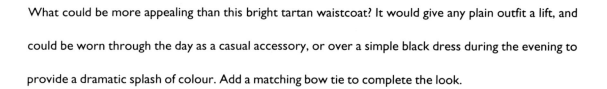

Choose a dressmaking pattern for a plain waistcoat, and cut out the two front sections from fusible interfacing. Cut out the front and back lining, and the back section, from fabric – you could select one of the ribbon colours, or stay with a more conventional black-satin lining.

Lay out the interfacing fronts, side by side, with the shiny (fusible) side upward. Take four tartan ribbons – three of 23 mm (⅞ in) in width and one of 75 mm (3 in) in width, and cut and place them at random over both fronts. Place the widest ribbon in position first, and then add the narrower ones haphazardly all round.

Adjust the ribbons until the arrangement looks good across both fronts, and pin to hold them in place. Carefully fuse the ribbons on to the interfacing, using an iron on a medium setting, and

This waistcoat with its front of bright tartan ribbons is very simple and quick to make.

then topstitch down the long edges of each.

To make up the waistcoat, first sew the front lining to each front section. Sew the front sections to the back, and then add the back lining to cover all raw edges. Finally, make buttonholes and sew on buttons.

To make a bow tie, cut a piece of fusible interfacing 36 cm (14 in) long by the width of the ribbon or ribbons. Fuse the ribbons on to the interfacing. With right sides facing, fold in the short ends to meet in the centre. Stitch the sides and turn the bow the right way out.

Repeat to make up a second bow piece.

For the strap, cut a 46 cm (18 in) length of ribbon. With wider ribbon, fold it in half lengthways, turn in the raw edges and topstitch all round; with narrower ribbon, cut and topstitch two lengths together, tucking in the raw ends. Lay out the strap, and place the two bows, right side outward, centrally on top of it. Bind the centre with a short strip of ribbon, and add a hook and eye to the ends of the strap to complete.

The white-spotted Swiss voile of the bodice on this dress is decorated with diagonal lengths of floral ribbon. Cut out the front and back bodice pieces from fusible interfacing, using a simple dressmaking pattern if you wish.

Lay the pieces out flat, with the shiny side upward. Lay 13 mm (½ in) wide embossed ribbons diagonally across the interfacing, with the edges butting together. Pin and fuse the ribbons in place. The ribbons are narrow, so there is no need to stitch them in place, but make sure that you have pressed them firmly. Stitch a fabric lining to the inside of the bodice.

Narrow ribbon embossed with tiny flower patterns is ideal for a little girl's party dress.

LITTLE MISS PRETTY

Party dresses must be pretty and feminine, and adding ribbon is the perfect way to enliven a plain dress or one that needs a new look. This practical pinafore is very quick to make, and slips over a dress to make a unique party outfit.

Cut out the skirt from fabric. The quickest way to neaten the side and hem edges is to turn them to the right side, lay a toning ribbon against the outer edge to cover the raw fabric edges, and topstitch it in place. Add a ribbon tie on either side of the skirt.

Softly gather the top edge of the skirt with running stitches, and sew it to the bodice, inserting lengths of ribbon into the seam at intervals. Make a fastening for the back bodice at the neck edge with a button and loop. Slip the finished pinafore over the child's head and fasten it at each side with the ribbon ties.

The ribboned bodice turns this simple pinafore into a pretty outfit, with co-ordinating ties and edging.

ONE STEP AHEAD

An elegant flower design in cream ribbon looks stunning on a black court shoe.

Put your best foot forward with these smart shoe trims. Plain shoes – whether destined for the beach or a party – look wonderful with the addition of ribbons and bows, while ribbon rosettes of all colours and sizes can be quickly made and anchored to the fronts of court shoes.

The contrast of cream against black creates the smart designer look on the left. Take seventeen 38 mm (1½ in) lengths of 32 mm (1¼ in) wide ribbon, and snip off the corners of each length to make a diamond shape. To form the petals, roll the long edges of the diamonds into the centre and secure each end with one or two tiny stitches.

Cut a 32 mm (1¼ in) diameter card circle, and glue the petals in place around the card.

Give espadrilles a

new lease of life

with pretty rosettes

(below). You could

add ribbon ties, too,

as a special touch.

Glue a black button in the centre to complete the flower. Make up a second flower in the same way, and fasten the card circles to shoe clips.

Transform espadrilles into gala evening wear with ribbon rosettes (below). Use 75 mm (3 in) wide sheer ribbon in the colours of your choice, fold it in half and then gather it up with running stitch along one edge to make the rosette (see page 11). Bunch the rosettes

together across the fronts of the espadrilles, and sew in place. Finally, if you wish, sew two lengths of 21 mm (¾ in) wide satin-ribbon ties to either side of the backs of the espadrilles.

To make the folded-ribbon rosette above, cut twenty-one 75 mm (3 in) lengths of 15 mm (⅝ in) wide bordered ribbon, and a 32 mm (1¼ in) diameter circle of card. Fold and press each length of ribbon in half, and glue one length overlapping the next around the card with the raw edges in the centre.

When the rosette is complete, glue a gilt button in the centre. Make a second rosette in the same way, and fasten the card circles to shoe clips.

Gold-edged ribbon

topped with a gilt

button creates a

sophisticated look

for shoes (above).

You could use bright

ribbon and buttons

for more casual

daywear.

Grosgrain ribbons in navy and a navy-and-white spot make up the elegant trim on the straw hat below. The ribbon used here is 38 mm (1½ in) wide, and you will need enough to go round your hat brim with a small overlap, plus approximately 51 cm (20 in) for the bow.

Stitch the two ribbons for the hat brim together, overlapping the spotted ribbon slightly to create a different width, and place them round the hat. For the bow, stitch the two

RIBBON HAT TRIMS

The stunning hat decoration above is easy to create. First cut a felt-circle base measuring 58 mm (2¼ in) in diameter. Cut nine 14 cm (5½ in) pieces of sheer blue ribbon, press them in half and stitch them to the felt in a half-fan arrangement.

Cut seven 10 cm (4 in) pieces of sheer print ribbon, iron them into petal shapes, and stitch them to the fan. Trim the centre with a blue-ribbon rose (see page 10). Cut a length of sheer print ribbon to fit round the hat, plus a small overlap, and sew the decoration over the join.

Transform your hats with colourful bands and unusual decoration. Combine prettily patterned ribbons with velvet, felt and straw to give each hat a new image – you could even run up several bands for each hat, and change them according to your outfit.

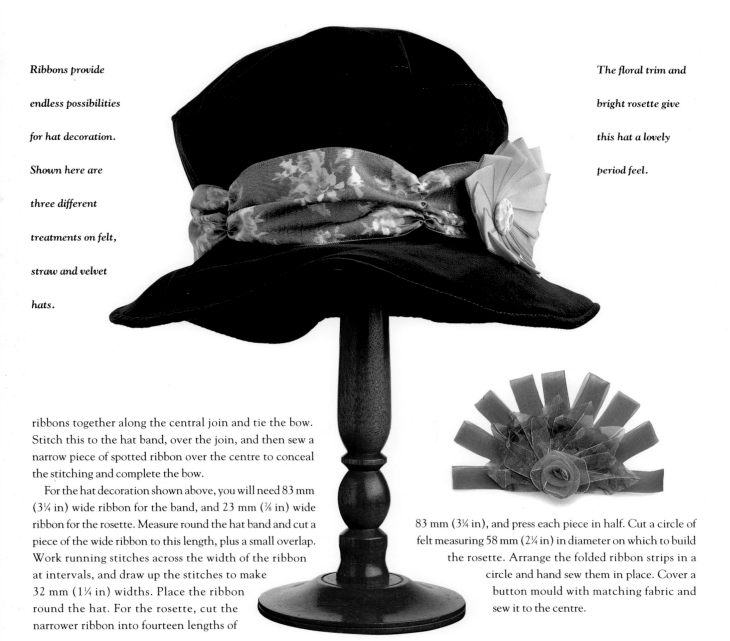

Ribbons provide endless possibilities for hat decoration. Shown here are three different treatments on felt, straw and velvet hats.

The floral trim and bright rosette give this hat a lovely period feel.

ribbons together along the central join and tie the bow. Stitch this to the hat band, over the join, and then sew a narrow piece of spotted ribbon over the centre to conceal the stitching and complete the bow.

For the hat decoration shown above, you will need 83 mm (3¼ in) wide ribbon for the band, and 23 mm (⅞ in) wide ribbon for the rosette. Measure round the hat band and cut a piece of the wide ribbon to this length, plus a small overlap. Work running stitches across the width of the ribbon at intervals, and draw up the stitches to make 32 mm (1¼ in) widths. Place the ribbon round the hat. For the rosette, cut the narrower ribbon into fourteen lengths of

83 mm (3¼ in), and press each piece in half. Cut a circle of felt measuring 58 mm (2¼ in) in diameter on which to build the rosette. Arrange the folded ribbon strips in a circle and hand sew them in place. Cover a button mould with matching fabric and sew it to the centre.

HAIR RIBBONS

An elegant slide of woven satin and velvet ribbons (above), and a colourful rosette on elastic (below).

A simple but striking ribbon design decorates this hair band.

Ribbons make ideal hair decorations. Instead of using them just to tie up pony tails and bunches, weave and create rosettes and clusters of gaily-coloured print and plain ribbons, and fix them to slides, bands and elastic straps for hair ornaments guaranteed to make every head turn in your direction.

To cover a plain slide such as the one shown above left, weave together narrow green satin and velvet ribbon. Cut four pieces of satin ribbon, each longer than the slide. Fasten them on the back, across one narrow end, and bring them round to the front. Secure the velvet ribbon at the back and start wrapping it round the slide. As you wrap, weave the satin ribbon under and over in a plain-weave formation. Secure the ends as at the start of the slide.

Double-sided print ribbon was used for the rosette on the left. Cut a 90 cm (36 in) length and turn under the cut ends, holding them with a zigzag stitch. Fold down one corner to make a point at one end. Sew a line of running stitch down the longer ribbon edge, catching down the folded corner. Gather up the ribbon tightly and fasten off the thread. Coil the ribbon around the pointed end, sewing the layers as you work. Sew the rosette to elastic.

Mix three 2 mm (1/12 in) ribbons to form the plaited hair band shown on the left. Cut 230 cm (90 in) lengths of each colour, and glue them side by side on the band, starting about 10 mm (3/8 in) from one end. Wrap the ribbons around the band, keeping them flat, in the correct order and as close together as possible. Glue the ends inside the band 10 mm (3/8 in) from the end. To highlight the centre, make a flat plait the length of the band and tuck the ends into the bound ribbon, three from the end on each side. Glue in place.

To make the loopy slide below, cut five 61 cm (24 in) lengths of sheer ribbon: two print, two dark pink and one green. Sandwich the five ribbons together, and wire them to the slide to create eight loops. Spread the ribbons apart to create fullness, and wind a piece of ribbon around the centre to complete the "bow".

For the comb on the right, cut two 34 cm (13¼ in) lengths of 35 mm (1⅜ in) wide Jacquard ribbon. Fold each length into a loop and sew the cut ends together. Lay the two loops side by side, with the seams at centre back, and gather up the loops on either side of the centre. Trim with a sheer ribbon rose (see page 10) and sew on to a hair comb.

The "caterpillar" slide below is easy to make. Cut a sheer ribbon and a narrower Jacquard ribbon three times longer than the slide. Lay the narrower ribbon centrally over the wider ribbon. Turn under the raw ends and sew a running stitch up the centre through both ribbons. Pull up the thread to gather the ribbon down the length of the slide, and work a few stitches at the end to secure the gather. Glue the ribbons to the slide.

A double bow and ribbon rose decorate a hair comb (above); and sheer and Jacquard ribbons make an attractive slide (below).

Pastel-coloured ribbons create lavish loops on this hair slide.

BAGS OF FUN

Woven, sewn or glued ribbons turn plain bags into spectacular accessories.

Pick strong ribbons in hot primary colours, and use them to create fun bags for the beach or to carry home your shopping. You can make your smart, new-look carriers as small or as large and vibrant as you like!

To make the purse bag on the left, cut a piece of fabric to 34 x16 cm (13½ x 6¼ in). Fold 21 cm (8¼ in) across the width, with right sides together, and stitch each side. Turn the right way out to form the bag and flap. Cut five lengths of ribbon and stitch them along the flap. Make a handle from a folded ribbon, and stitch this on either side of the bag. Sew a piece of ribbon inside the flap, and a corresponding piece on the bag, to fasten the flap.

For the duffle bag opposite, cut a piece of strong fabric to 66 x 42 cm (26 x 16½ in) for the bag side. Choose three ribbons, cut each in half, and stitch them to each side of the fabric. Fold the fabric and join the side seam, then cut a 20 cm (8 in) diameter fabric base and stitch this to the side piece. Turn the bag the right way out and bind the top edge. Stitch a casing below the ribbons at the top, leaving a gap on either side. Cut two lengths of 10 mm (⅜ in) wide ribbon and thread each through the casing. Knot the ends, and pull up the ribbons for ties.

To make the shopping bag, cut two pieces of woven fusible interfacing and backing fabric, each 32 x 45 cm (12½ x 17¾ in). Lay the interfacing flat, with the shiny side up. Weave ribbons over the interfacing and fuse in place. Fold with right sides together and, leaving the top open, stitch to the backing fabric. Turn the right way out, neaten the top edge and add ribbon handles.

PRETTY PURSES

Keep your small change or make-up in a pretty ribbon purse.

Ribbon also makes an ideal decoration on tiny drawstring

bags, for special evening purses. Match the ribbon colours to

your favourite outfit, or make several

bags for different occasions!

A simple criss-cross

pattern looks

attractive on this

make-up purse.

Choose a plain-fabric background for this make-up purse. Cut out two pieces of fabric measuring 15 x 27 cm (6 x 10½ in). Topstitch ribbon diagonally in each direction across each piece. Turn under the seam allowance along the top edges, and sew each edge to one half of a zip. Stitch all round the remaining three sides, trim the edges and turn the purse to the right side through the zip.

The little bag on the right is very quick to make. Cut two pieces of fusible interfacing to 19 x 13 cm (7½ x 5 in). On each piece, lay patterned ribbons in bands across the shape, adding a plain extra-wide ribbon at the base. Stitch a casing made from a 38 mm (1½ in) wide ribbon to the right side, 50 mm (2 in) from the top.

Use a small plate as a template to round off the bottom edges on each piece, place the right sides together and

The "fabric" of

these little bags is

made entirely of

ribbons, with

tasselled cords to

pull them up.

stitch all round, leaving the top edge open. Turn under the top edge and stitch a narrow hem. Turn the bag the right way out. Thread cord through the casing and add a tassel to each end.

To make the bag on the left, cut a piece of fusible interfacing 38 x 30 cm (15 x 12 in). Lay it flat with the shiny side up. Lay 10 mm (⅜ in) wide patterned ribbons lengthways over the whole piece, and fuse in place. Fold the raw top edges to the outside, and bind with 23 mm (⅞ in) wide ribbon. Add a casing of the same ribbon on the right side of the fabric, 8 cm (3¼ in) from the top edge. Fold the fabric in half with the right sides together and seam. Cut an 11 cm (4¼ in) diameter circle of fabric and stitch this into the base. Thread cord through the casing and add a tassel to complete.

31

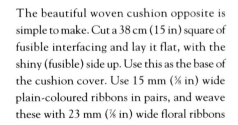

The beautiful woven cushion opposite is simple to make. Cut a 38 cm (15 in) square of fusible interfacing and lay it flat, with the shiny (fusible) side up. Use this as the base of the cushion cover. Use 15 mm (⅝ in) wide plain-coloured ribbons in pairs, and weave these with 23 mm (⅞ in) wide floral ribbons

CUSHION COMFORTS

Your ideas for cushion covers will be endless when you see the vast selection of ribbons from which to choose. The décor of a room will usually dictate the colour, but you can still pick your ribbons from many patterned and textured varieties. You could link a series of cushions, giving each one its own stamp with a different weave or ribbon arrangement.

Plain and floral

ribbons create a

lovely effect on the

cushion opposite.

See pages 12-13 for

examples of basic

weaves and

instructions.

to create the pattern shown here. When the design looks good and is tightly woven, fuse the ribbons in place using a medium-hot iron. To ensure that the ribbons will hold, turn over the interfacing and press it again on the wrong side.

The diagonally woven cover overleaf is made up in the same way as the first cushion, but the weave is different. Lay half

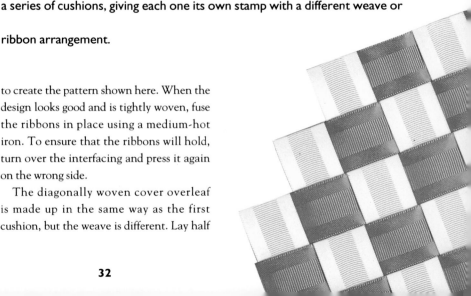

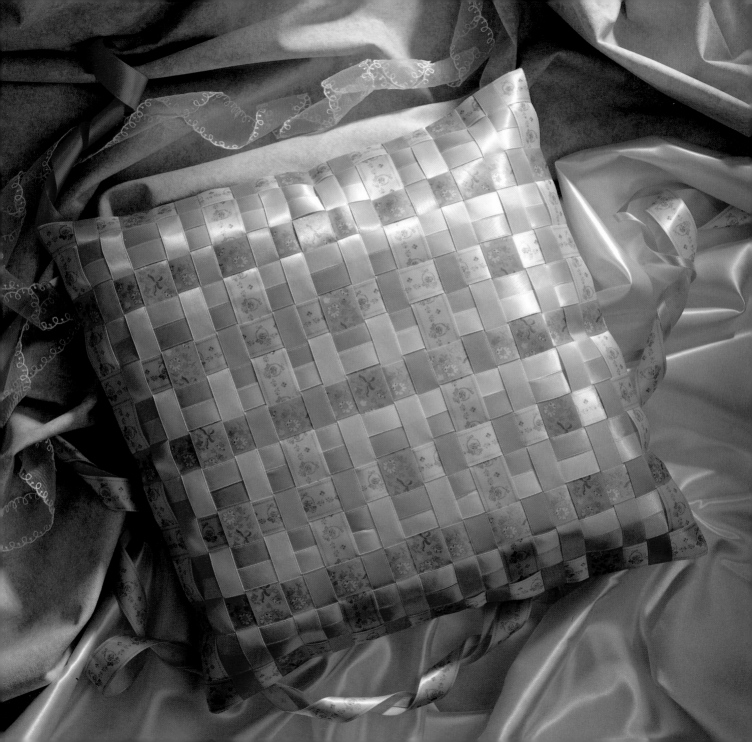

the ribbons diagonally across the interfacing, then tightly weave the remaining ribbons vertically over the interfacing. Fuse the ribbons in position, again pressing from both sides to achieve a firm fabric.

Overlapping diagonal ribbons make an attractive design on the cushion opposite (top). Cut a 38 cm (15 in) square of fusible interfacing and lay it flat, with the shiny side up. Use a combination of cream, rust and peach ribbons in 38 mm (1½ in), 32 mm (1¼ in) and 15 mm (⅝ in) widths to work the pattern. Lay the ribbons diagonally across the interfacing in both directions, as shown to create the design. Fuse the ribbons in place and, to hold them firmly, topstitch each one along the outer edges. Add definition to the central pattern with a border made with the rust-coloured ribbon. Pin this in position, and then topstitch the edges to hold the ribbon securely in place.

Toning ribbons

woven diagonally

create the eye-

catching design

shown on the left.

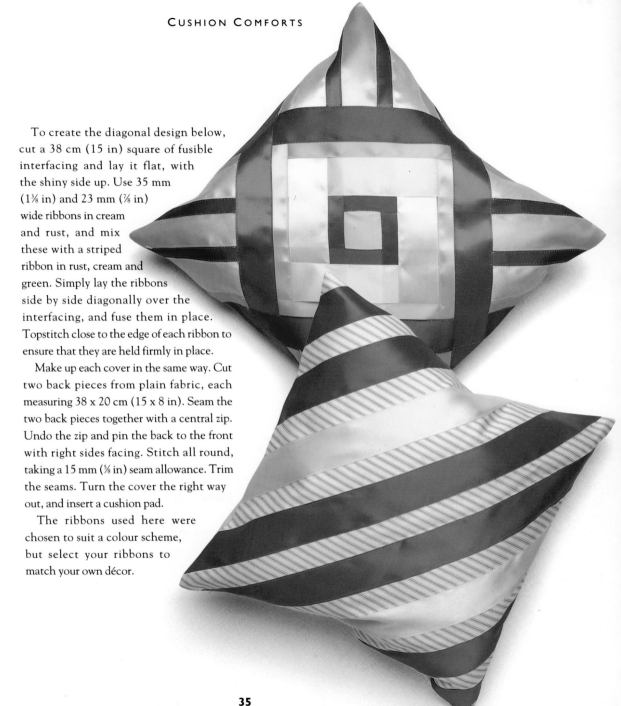

To create the diagonal design below, cut a 38 cm (15 in) square of fusible interfacing and lay it flat, with the shiny side up. Use 35 mm (1⅜ in) and 23 mm (⅞ in) wide ribbons in cream and rust, and mix these with a striped ribbon in rust, cream and green. Simply lay the ribbons side by side diagonally over the interfacing, and fuse them in place. Topstitch close to the edge of each ribbon to ensure that they are held firmly in place.

Make up each cover in the same way. Cut two back pieces from plain fabric, each measuring 38 x 20 cm (15 x 8 in). Seam the two back pieces together with a central zip. Undo the zip and pin the back to the front with right sides facing. Stitch all round, taking a 15 mm (⅝ in) seam allowance. Trim the seams. Turn the cover the right way out, and insert a cushion pad.

The ribbons used here were chosen to suit a colour scheme, but select your ribbons to match your own décor.

(Right) an elegant

pair of cushions

created with

striking designs in

rust, pink and

cream ribbons.

The ribbon decoration across the corner of the pillowcase on the left is simple but very attractive. Cut 10 mm (⅜ in) wide ribbon into five graduating lengths and topstitch them in place diagonally across one corner, leaving evenly spaced gaps between each

A simple ribbon design such as the one on the left transforms a plain pillowcase.

SWEET DREAMS

Plain bedlinen looks marvellous with motif additions, and pillowcases are the obvious target because they are quick to decorate. Match similar ribbon colours and pillowcases, and use pretty picot-edged ribbons to provide that distinctive touch.

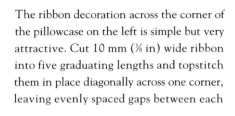

ribbon and turning under the raw edges neatly. You could add more ribbon rows if you wish, but these may become awkward to sew as you move away from the open edge of the pillowcase, unless you sew them by hand rather than machine.

To create the design on this cream pillowcase, cut a length of picot-edged dark ribbon, to contrast with the background, and pin it to the open end of your pillowcase, 50 mm (2 in) from the edge. Stitch the ribbon in place. Next, cut a piece of narrower, cream-coloured ribbon into 36 cm (14 in) and 64 cm (25¼ in) lengths.

Beginning at the bottom of the pillowcase, position the 36 cm (14 in) length centrally over the wider ribbon, and stitch it in place for 10 cm (4 in). At the top, stitch the 64 cm (25¼ in) length of ribbon centrally over the wider ribbon for 34 cm (13¼ in). Tie the trailing ends of the ribbon into a bow, between the two sewn strips.

For the navy pillowcase, cut one length of decorative ribbon and pin this along the open end of a pillowcase, 10 cm (4 in) from the edge. Cut short lengths of the same ribbon and pin them diagonally from the pillowcase edge to the ribbon band, as shown. Tuck the inner raw ends under the ribbon band, and turn under the opposite ends in line with the pillowcase edge. Tack and then topstitch the ribbons in place to secure them firmly.

Ribbon tied in a bow gives a feminine look to a cream pillowcase (above), while a geometric pattern suits a navy background.

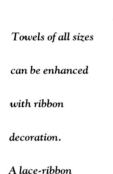

Towels of all sizes

can be enhanced

with ribbon

decoration.

A lace-ribbon

TRIMMED TOWELS

The pretty lace bow shown above is perfect for a small hand towel. Take a piece of 38 mm (1½ in) wide lace ribbon measuring the length of the towel plus about 20 cm (8 in) for the bow. Cut the ribbon into a short and a longer length. Turning under the raw ends, pin and stitch one piece along the woven border on the towel from the left-hand edge and the other piece from the right-hand edge, leaving 10 cm (4 in) of each ribbon unstitched. Tie these ends into a bow and catch with a few hand stitches to secure.

bow gives a pretty

finish to the powder-

blue hand towel

shown above.

Brighten up bathtime with beribboned towels. Pastel towels especially benefit from the addition of ornamental bands of ribbons. Use the ribbon shades to tie together an assortment of different-coloured towels into one attractive colour scheme to suit your décor.

For the zigzag design on the right, cut a length of 10 mm (⅜ in) wide picot-edged ribbon and fold it into a zigzag pattern along the woven border of the towel. Turn under the raw ends to neaten, and tack and topstitch in place.

To create the stripes below, cut a length of 10 mm (⅜ in) wide picot-edged ribbon in half lengthways, and tack one piece to each side of insertion lace. Stitch this in place along the woven towel border, turning under the raw ends to neaten.

For the "helter-skelter" design on the pink towel, wrap 10 mm (⅜ in) wide picot-edged ribbon around 35 mm (1⅜ in) wide lace ribbon to form a diagonal pattern. Stitch this in position. Stitch the ribbon along the woven border of the towel, turning under the raw ends to neaten them.

Ribbons are perfect

for co-ordinating

bathroom

accessories, as

this small set of

pastel towels shows.

Add sophistication to your table with smart ribbon-trimmed napkins, such as the one shown below.

TASTEFUL TABLE-LINEN

Plain ribbons look beautiful on smart table-linen. Make up a set of napkins with a table-cloth to match, or use your ingenuity to decorate the edges of each napkin with a different design. Weave the ribbons together at the corners or create a single striking motif – the choice is yours.

The possibilities for decorating napkins with ribbons are almost limitless. Shown on the left and opposite are two examples which are easy to make but look stunning. For the napkin on the left, cut and pin a length of 10 mm (⅜ in) wide picot-edged ribbon to fit along each side, 38 mm (1½ in) inside the outer edge. Pin a second length of ribbon 21 mm (¾ in) inside the first ribbon. Weave the ribbons together at the corners where they cross. Tack and topstitch the ribbons in place, stitching along both edges for a secure finish that will withstand laundering.

To make the design shown opposite, cut a length of 38 mm (1½ in) wide ribbon to fit along three sides of the napkin. Pin the ribbon in place, mitring the corners neatly and concealing the raw edges. Tack and then topstitch the ribbon, stitching along both edges.

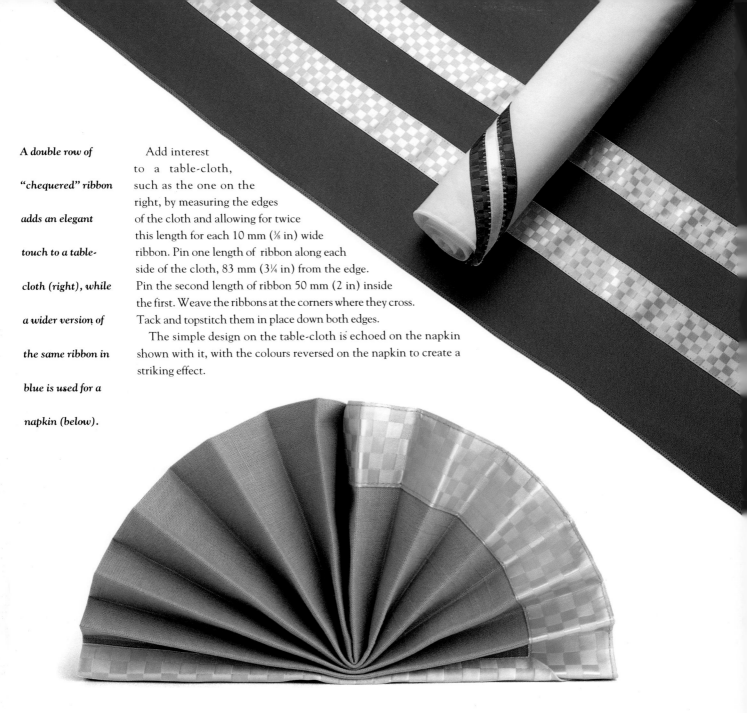

A double row of "chequered" ribbon adds an elegant touch to a table-cloth (right), while a wider version of the same ribbon in blue is used for a napkin (below).

Add interest to a table-cloth, such as the one on the right, by measuring the edges of the cloth and allowing for twice this length for each 10 mm (⅜ in) wide ribbon. Pin one length of ribbon along each side of the cloth, 83 mm (3¼ in) from the edge. Pin the second length of ribbon 50 mm (2 in) inside the first. Weave the ribbons at the corners where they cross. Tack and topstitch them in place down both edges.

The simple design on the table-cloth is echoed on the napkin shown with it, with the colours reversed on the napkin to create a striking effect.

The dainty bon-bonnière shown on the left would look attractive on any table. Cut a 28 cm (11 in) square of fine net and topstitch a narrow picot-edged ribbon around the outer edge. Place a few sugared almonds in the centre and tie up the net with two lengths of ribbon – one pink, one white – and into a bow. Trim the ribbon ends diagonally.

A pretty pink-and-white colour scheme has been used for the stunning display opposite.

Sugared almonds in a beribboned bon-bonnière (above) make a charming little present for wedding guests.

CHAMPAGNE RECEPTION

For the stunning table-cloth opposite, measure the table top and add 41 cm (16 in) to this diameter for an overhang. Cut a circle of plain white cotton fabric to this size. Neaten the edge and topstitch a length of narrow picot-edged ribbon around it.

Next, divide the cloth into six equal sections, and, at each of these points, work two rows of gathering stitches up to the table edge. Pull up the cloth and tie off the threads. Tie lengths of wire-edged ribbon into extravagant bows, and hand sew one over each gathered row.

Weave a magical spell around a wedding reception with beautiful ribbons. Combine embossed and sheer ribbons to make pretty candle holders, napkin rings and a ring cushion, and tie lavish bows to a ruched table-cloth to create a spectacular table setting.

To make the delicate ring cushion below, cut two pieces of white cotton fabric, each 23 cm (9 in) square. On the front piece, add a border of 38 mm (1½ in) wide embossed ribbon 15 mm (⅝ in) from the outer edge. Mitre the corners neatly to fit. Add a second border of 32 mm (1¼ in) wide embossed ribbon inside the first, this time overlapping the edges at the corners to form a neat edge. Topstitch both ribbons in place.

Gather up a sheer white-edged ribbon twice the length of the outer edge.

Spacing the gathers evenly, pin and tack this around the outer edge. With right sides facing, pin and stitch the back to the front, leaving an opening in one side. Trim and turn the cover the right way out, insert a pad and oversew the opening. Tie a bow of picot-edged ribbon at each corner, and a slightly larger one in the centre, to hold the rings, and sew them in place.

To make the unusual candle holder opposite, first cut a 15 cm (6 in) diameter circle of card, and stick a paper doily over the top. For the outer edge, cut 20 cm (8 in) lengths of white embossed 35 mm (1⅜ in) wide ribbon. Fold each length into a petal shape, and glue the petals around the ring in pairs, spacing them evenly. Glue two 20 cm (8 in) loops of extra-wide sheer ribbon in between each pair.

For the second layer, make up five large flowers from plain sheer ribbon. To do this, fold a long length of extra-wide sheer ribbon into petals, layering them one on top of the other to form the flower. Space the flowers evenly around the card and glue them in place, adding a large "pearl" in the centre of each. Leave the centre of the arrangement free for the candle holder of your choice.

This exquisite ring cushion (below left) has embossed-ribbon borders, ribbons at the centre and corners, and a sheer edging ribbon.

Make the matching napkin ring by stitching two 23 cm (9 in) lengths of 40 mm (1½ in) wide white embossed ribbon into rings. Place these back to back with a layer of interfacing in between, and topstitch them together around the outer edges. Form a white ribbon loop on each side and stitch them in place. Make up a sheer flower with a pearl centre, following the instructions given for the candle holder, and then hand sew the flower to the napkin ring to cover the joins.

The sheer cream ribbon used for this candle holder looks beautiful in the glow of the candle flame.

This delicate napkin ring (above) matches the candle holder beautifully to make a perfect table setting.

The photograph frame opposite is easily made. First, cover your chosen frame with velvet. Dark green has been used here to match the other accessories, but you could of course use any colour of velvet. Make up two pale pink, one dark pink and one cream rose from satin ribbon, and arrange these on the frame. Wrap the stems together, finishing with a dark pink bow and adding leaves.

The first step in making the coat-hanger shown above is to bind round the hook with cream ribbon. Next, measure the length of the hanger and allow for twice this length, and measure round the hanger and add a 15 mm (⅝ in) seam allowance. Cut a piece of green velvet to these measurements. Fold the velvet round the hanger, turn in the allowance and pin the folded edges together. Gather up the folded edge from each side and fasten off.

Make two rosettes in each pink ribbon by working a running stitch along one edge and gathering the ribbon into folds (see page 11). Tie a length of cream ribbon round the hook so that the ends hang down, and glue two rosettes back to back round each end. Make three roses (see page 10) in each colour, and stitch them round the hook.

COMING UP ROSES

Try making this colourful set of co-ordinating trinkets — combining luxurious velvet fabric with cream and pink rosebuds and rosettes — for your bedroom. These attractive pieces would make wonderful presents, too, and each one can easily be run up in an evening.

The extravagant coathanger opposite will add luxury to any wardrobe, and is fit for the best of clothes.

Glue the arrangement to one corner of the frame, as shown.

Lavish ribbon rosettes look wonderful on the lid of a velvet-coated jewellery box (below). If you do not already have a box of this type, you will be able to buy one fairly cheaply, or you could make your own by lining and covering a suitable box with velvet. To add the lid decoration, make up five cream, five pale pink and five dark pink rosettes. Glue these haphazardly on the box lid, and add a few folded ribbon leaves between the flower shapes to finish.

Velvet and ribbon make a beautiful combination on this elegant matching photograph frame and jewellery box.

BOWS, BOWS, BOWS

Ribbon can be stiffened into shapes with specialist

solutions or a diluted PVA adhesive. Arrange the

ribbons, then simply paint over both sides with

the glue mixture. The ribbon will stiffen

and remain in the fixed

shapes, as well as gaining

a shiny surface that

creates an attractive effect.

Stiffened ribbon has

many uses – the frame

and plant pot on this

page are just two ideas.

Use a coloured photograph mount as the base for the frame shown on the opposite page. Cut a length of reversible green-and-red gold-edged ribbon, and tie a bow in the centre. Coat both sides of the ribbon with diluted adhesive, and then stick the bow to the top of the mount. Stick the ribbon ends to either side of the frame in loops, using pins to hold them until they are completely dry.

Woven plant pots look very attractive with a ribbon trim. To make the design shown on the left, allow for one-and-a-half times the diameter of the pot top, and cut a piece of extra-wide ribbon to this length. Fold it in half over the pot edge and pin. Tie a large bow and sew this to the basket, over the ribbon join. Coat both the ribbon edge and the bow with diluted adhesive and leave to dry.

The decoration on the cane wreath above is simple but looks very effective. Bind round the wreath with red-and-white gingham ribbon, and fasten it at the top. Cut a length of the same ribbon, tie this into a bow and attach it to the top of the wreath. Cut the ribbon ends diagonally, leaving them to trail. Make a ribbon rose and fasten it over

Red-and-white

gingham ribbon tied

in an extravagant

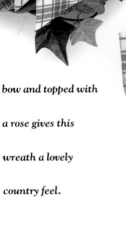

bow and topped with

a rose gives this

wreath a lovely

country feel.

the bow. Paint the ribbons with diluted adhesive and leave them to dry, and then intertwine greenery or dried flowers as you wish.

The little basket below uses the same ribbon as the wreath. Bind the basket handle, and tie lengths of ribbon into bows on either side. Cut the ends diagonally. Stiffen the ribbon with diluted adhesive and leave it to dry thoroughly.

The same gingham

ribbon transforms

the woven basket

below. A wide floral

ribbon would also

look pretty.

Luxurious floral-and-gold ribbon creates a stunning arrangement. Poppyseed heads sprayed with gold complete the rich effect.

Dried hydrangea heads and gold-sprayed poppyseed heads were chosen to complement the beautiful gold-backed floral ribbon in the posy on the left. To make this up, first bind the plant stems with wire, and then make a four-loop bow. Begin by forming two loops in a conventional bow shape, finishing with the remaining length of ribbon on the top to make a "cross" in the centre. (Don't worry about the neatness of the bows at this stage, as these can be adjusted at the end.)

Hold the loops in place with your thumb and forefinger. Make a third and fourth loop in the same way, bringing the end of the ribbon over the middle of the bow once again to make a second cross, and leaving one long end to trail. Cut the ribbon ends on

WIRED BOWS

A shiny, patterned ribbon makes an eye-catching wreath (right).

Wire-edged ribbon is wonderful for creating lavish bows, as it is easy to mould and retains its shape indefinitely. You can use wire-edged ribbon throughout a design, or you could remove part of the wire and make trailing streamers to complement crisp wired bows.

a slant to neaten them. Ease the bow into shape so that the loops cover the central binding wire.

The small bouquet on this page looks beautiful with its delicate bow of gold-edged cream ribbon. To make it up, first bind your chosen flower stems with wire. Create the six-loop bow by following the previous instructions for a four-loop bow, adding the fifth and sixth loops in the same way.

Bind the centre of the bow with fine wire, and then pin a strip of ribbon over it to resemble a self-tie.

This delicate bouquet would make a lovely posy for a bride or bridesmaid, perhaps with matching flowers for the hair.

Adjust the loops until they make nice round shapes, and then thread a wire through the back of the bow and twist it round the flower stems. For the "streamers", attach a length of ribbon, just off-centre, to a wire, and then join this to the stems. Neaten the ribbon ends by cutting them at an angle.

A six-loop bow was also used on the small wreath opposite, with two of the loops snipped through to make four trailing ends.

Make the little heart sachet on the left by
cutting picot-edged ribbon in two colours
into 13 cm (5 in) lengths. Cut a 13 cm
(5 in) square of fusible interfacing, and lay
this shiny side up. Weave the ribbons to
form a fabric (see pages 12-13), and fuse
them in place. Cut out a heart shape from
this ribbon fabric, and also from muslin or
thin cotton backing fabric. Place the fabrics
with right sides together, and pin and stitch all round,

Ribbons add the

perfect touch to tiny

pot-pourri sachets.

Muslin allows the

perfume to escape.

SCENTED SACHETS

Pretty pastel sachets are perfect to slip between
your clothes to keep them smelling sweet. Fill each
one with your favourite pot pourri to create a
lovely fragrance.

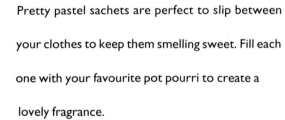

Picot-edged ribbons

in pink and cream

are perfect for a

little sachet (above).

leaving an opening. Trim the seam and turn the fabric
the right way out. Fill the heart with pot pourri and
oversew the opening. Sew on ribbon loops to hang up
the heart, and add a small ribbon rose to complete.

The three sachets opposite are easy to make. For the
"sack" shape, cut two pieces of muslin to 34 x 10 cm (13¼
x 4 in) and stitch floral picot-edged ribbon diagonally
across the two bottom corners on each piece of muslin.
Stitch the two pieces together on three sides, leaving the
fourth (short) side open. Trim the seams and turn the
right way out. Fold down 7 mm (¼ in) around the top
edge and stitch matching ribbon around the top to cover
this raw edge. Fill the bag with pot pourri and tie it up
with ribbon.

For the pillow, cut a piece of fusible interfacing
measuring 12 x 14 cm (4½ x 5½ in). Cut two different
ribbons into 10 cm (4 in) lengths. Overlapping the edges
and alternating the ribbons, fuse them to the interfacing.
With right sides together, stitch the ribbon fabric to
muslin backing fabric, leaving an opening. Trim the
seam, turn and fill with pot pourri. Slipstitch the opening.

To make the parcel, cut two pieces of muslin, each
measuring 12 x 14 cm (4½ x 5½ in). Cut a piece of lace
ribbon to match, and tack to each piece of muslin. Place
right sides together, pin and stitch, leaving an opening.
Trim the seam and turn, then fill with pot pourri and
slipstitch the opening. Use two 70 cm (27½ in) lengths of
ribbon to tie the muslin up like a parcel.

LAVENDER BOTTLES

Lavender bottles woven with ribbons make beautiful little gifts.

Bottles of long-stemmed lavender, woven with ribbons, will scent all your linen beautifully. Layer the bottles between the sheets in your linen chest or airing cupboard, or hang them in any position where their delicate fragrance will be appreciated.

Choose lavender with long stalks and pick approximately fifteen stems, making sure that they are all similar in thickness and length. Harvest the lavender when it is ripe and in the morning so that any dew will have dried.

Tie the lavender stalks together just under the heads, with one end of a 200 cm (80 in) length of 3 mm (⅛ in) wide ribbon. Bend the stalks back on themselves and fan them out round the heads to create enough space for weaving the ribbon. Next, thread the longer ribbon end on to a blunt tapestry needle, and use this to

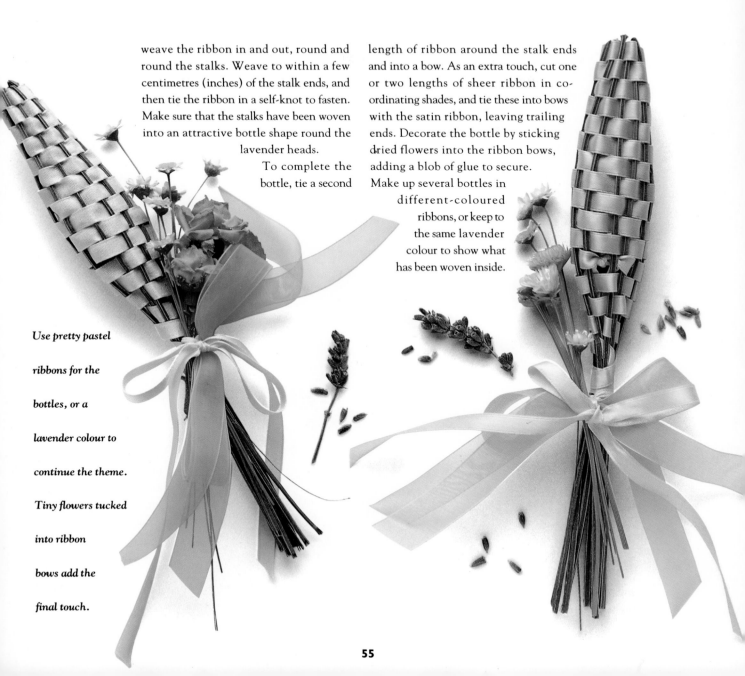

weave the ribbon in and out, round and round the stalks. Weave to within a few centimetres (inches) of the stalk ends, and then tie the ribbon in a self-knot to fasten. Make sure that the stalks have been woven into an attractive bottle shape round the lavender heads.

To complete the bottle, tie a second length of ribbon around the stalk ends and into a bow. As an extra touch, cut one or two lengths of sheer ribbon in co-ordinating shades, and tie these into bows with the satin ribbon, leaving trailing ends. Decorate the bottle by sticking dried flowers into the ribbon bows, adding a blob of glue to secure. Make up several bottles in different-coloured ribbons, or keep to the same lavender colour to show what has been woven inside.

Use pretty pastel ribbons for the bottles, or a lavender colour to continue the theme. Tiny flowers tucked into ribbon bows add the final touch.

STUNNING STOCKINGS

Get into the Christmas spirit with these delightful felt stockings. Each one uses glittery ribbons for the decoration, and is very simple to put together. Make a loop at the back and hang the stocking on the mantelpiece or bed end, all ready for Santa's presents.

Draw up a pattern for a stocking 41 cm (16 in) long and 17 cm (6½ in) wide, copying the shape of a sock or a picture. When the stocking looks realistic, cut out the pattern, and then use this to cut out two stocking pieces from felt.

To make the first stocking, cut two Christmas ribbons into lengths, lay them alternately and diagonally across one stocking piece, and pin and topstitch them in position. Place the stocking pieces with right sides facing, and pin and stitch them together all round, leaving the top edge open. Turn the right way out.

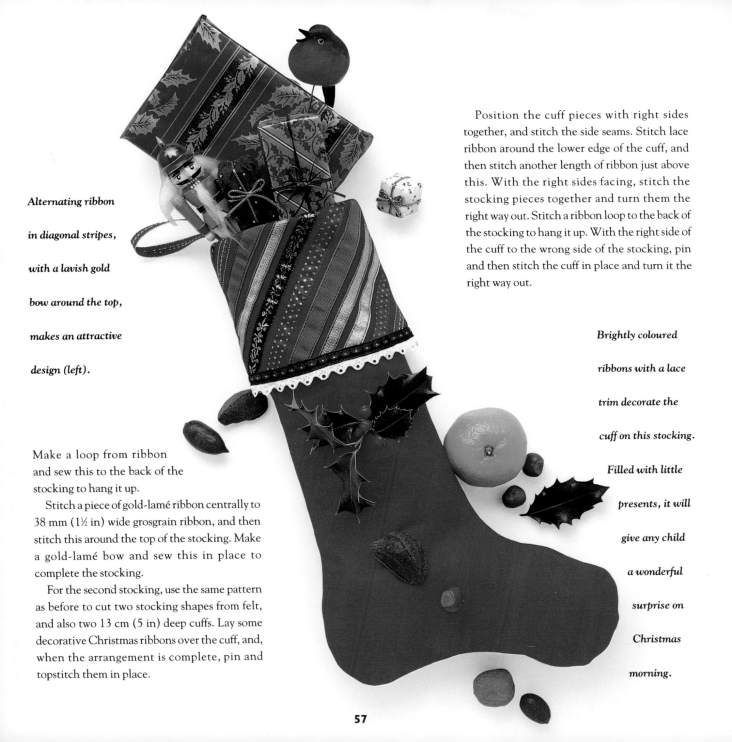

Alternating ribbon

in diagonal stripes,

with a lavish gold

bow around the top,

makes an attractive

design (left).

Position the cuff pieces with right sides together, and stitch the side seams. Stitch lace ribbon around the lower edge of the cuff, and then stitch another length of ribbon just above this. With the right sides facing, stitch the stocking pieces together and turn them the right way out. Stitch a ribbon loop to the back of the stocking to hang it up. With the right side of the cuff to the wrong side of the stocking, pin and then stitch the cuff in place and turn it the right way out.

Brightly coloured

ribbons with a lace

trim decorate the

cuff on this stocking.

Filled with little

presents, it will

give any child

a wonderful

surprise on

Christmas

morning.

Make a loop from ribbon and sew this to the back of the stocking to hang it up.

Stitch a piece of gold-lamé ribbon centrally to 38 mm (1½ in) wide grosgrain ribbon, and then stitch this around the top of the stocking. Make a gold-lamé bow and sew this in place to complete the stocking.

For the second stocking, use the same pattern as before to cut two stocking shapes from felt, and also two 13 cm (5 in) deep cuffs. Lay some decorative Christmas ribbons over the cuff, and, when the arrangement is complete, pin and topstitch them in place.

To make the hanging ball shown opposite, cut an 80 cm (31½ in) length of gold-lamé ribbon and thread it through the centre of a polystyrene ball. Knot the ends together at the base (the rest of the ribbon will form the hanging loop).

Cut 25 cm (10 in) lengths of the following ribbons: 10 mm (⅜ in) wide red-and-gold ribbon, 10 mm (⅜ in) wide red-and-green ribbon, 13 mm (½ in) wide gold-lamé ribbon, 25 mm (1 in) wide green-tartan ribbon and 25 mm (1 in) wide red-tartan ribbon.

Fold each length of ribbon into three loops. Bind the centres of the loops with florists' wire, and twist the ends together. Push the ends

CHRISTMAS COLOUR

Bring a touch of individuality to Christmas with your own decorations. This hanging bauble and stunning candle holder would add elegance to any table setting.

The beautiful decorations opposite can be made up in any colour combination to suit your décor, and used year after year.

into the polystyrene ball. Wrap wire round the bases of several pine cones, and wind the ends together. Push the ends into different parts of the ball to complete the arrangement.

Make the base of the candle holder by binding a 15 cm (6 in) diameter polystyrene ring with 6 mm (¼ in) wide green ribbon, overlapping the edges in the centre and spreading them out around the outer edge.

Make up simple rosettes of green, gold-lamé and red ribbons by working running stitch along one edge of each ribbon and pulling it up (see page 11). Glue the rosettes evenly around the ring. Finally, make some bows from tartan ribbon, and glue these and a few pine cones and seed pods between the rosettes.

Ribbon loops, bows and rosettes, interspersed with pine cones and seed pods, create a wonderfully festive feel.

LABOUR OF LOVE

Ensure that your message of true love is received loud and clear on 14 February by making your own Valentine's card. Your card will be totally original, and the traditional red ribbons and heart shapes will show the object of your affection that you really care. Both of the cards shown here are very simple to make, or you could come up with your own variation.

To make the pretty roses card on the left, cut a piece of card to 46 x 21 cm (18 x 18¼ in). Score across the card on both sides, 15 cm (6 in) and 30 cm (12 in) from one short edge to make three sections (these will fold in a "concertina" shape later to make the finished card shape). Mark a 25 mm (1 in) border all round the front section of the card, and cut out the centre. Take a piece of pink paper measuring 21 x 15 cm (8¼ x 6 in) and glue this to the second section of the card.

Make up four roses using 35 cm (13¾ in) of 10 mm (⅜ in) wide velvet ribbon. Draw the rose stems and leaves on the card, and then glue the roses in position. Make a bow from 15 mm (⅝ in) wide heart-print ribbon, and glue it in place. Fold up the card. Add decoration

A home-made

ribbon card, rather

than a shop-bought

card, makes a

really personal

Valentine's-day gift

for someone special.

around the border with gold pen or stick-on motifs if you wish.

To make the sheer-heart card opposite, cut a piece of card to the same size as the roses card, and score it across in the same way. On another piece of paper, draw a heart shape just under the size of the card. To make sure that the heart is symmetrical, fold the paper in half down the centre of the heart, and then cut around the outer edge. Unfold the paper, place the heart shape on the card and mark round it carefully. Cut out the heart from the front two sections of the card, and make a slit on either side of the heart in the front section only.

Glue 50 mm (2 in) wide sheer ribbon in position behind the front heart. Slot 20 mm (¾ in) wide satin ribbon into the slits, glue on the wrong side to secure, and then fold and glue it in place on the front, as shown. Glue the first and second sections of the card together, and fold it up.

PAPER MAGIC

Paper ribbons come in many different widths and colours, and each variation can be twisted and tied into attractive arrangements. Unwrap and spread out the wide ribbon, and use it to bind round basket handles and boxes. Pull the thinner craft ribbon against scissor blades to make it curl and wave in wonderful ways.

Paper ribbon makes beautiful ties for gift-wrapping. Here, cream and ivy-coloured ribbons combined with plain brown paper create a lovely natural feel.

Parcels wrapped in ordinary brown paper look stunning when decorated with paper ribbon in toning colours. To decorate the round box, unravel the paper ribbon and make two bows – the larger one from green ribbon, and the smaller one from cream ribbon. Lay the cream bow on top of the green one and bind the centre with a small band of green ribbon. Stick the bows centrally to the top of the box and decorate it with nuts to complete the rustic effect.

The decoration on the square box is also very simple. Wrap once round the box with a strip of green ribbon. Tie the ends of the ribbon

Simple paper-ribbon

flowers adorn the

top of this pretty

wreath, with more

ribbon wrapped

around it and

flowers tucked

inside.

together, and then unravel the centre section of each end piece, leaving the ends tightly twisted to create a "leaf" shape. Tie a length of cream ribbon at right angles to the green ribbon, and unravel the centres of the end sections in the same way.

The wreath shown above would look attractive in any kitchen. To make it up, first wind round a basic cane wreath with narrow craft paper ribbon. Work diagonally around the wreath once, and then go around again, overlapping the previous ribbon in a criss-cross fashion. Tie lengths of the same ribbon around the bound ribbons at intervals, and curl the ends by pulling a scissor blade along them.

Make two paper flowers by cutting out petal shapes from unravelled paper ribbon. Bind the petals together around short lengths of tightly twisted ribbon to form stamens. Glue in beads to make the centres, and stick the flowers to the top of the wreath. Glue on pine cones and nuts, and weave in odd flowers as you wish.

ACKNOWLEDGMENTS

The author would like to thank the following for their help with the ribbon projects:
Caroline Birkett-Harris, Penny Hill, Beryl Miller and Pamela Westland.

Quarto would also like to thank the following for kindly providing ribbons for the
projects in this book:

Mokuba Co., Ltd, 4-16-8 Kuramae, Taito-ku, Tokyo, Japan. Phone: 81-3-3864-7700.
Fax: 81-3-3864-4013.
C.M. Offray & Son Ltd. Phone: 0784-247281.
Panda ribbons from *Selectus Ltd*, Biddulph, Stoke-on-Trent ST8 7RH.
Phone: 0782-522316.